Little RIDDLERS

Scottish Verses

Edited By Machaela Gavaghan

First published in Great Britain in 2018 by:

Young**Writers**

Young Writers
Remus House
Coltsfoot Drive
Peterborough
PE2 9BF
Telephone: 01733 890066
Website: www.youngwriters.co.uk

FOREWORD

Dear Reader,

Are you ready to get your thinking caps on to puzzle your way through this wonderful collection?

Young Writers' Little Riddlers competition set out to encourage young writers to create their own riddles. Their answers could be whatever or whoever their imaginations desired; from people to places, animals to objects, food to seasons. Riddles are a great way to further the children's use of poetic expression, including onomatopoeia and similes, as well as encourage them to 'think outside the box' by providing clues without giving the answer away immediately.

All of us here at Young Writers believe in the importance of inspiring young children to produce creative writing, including poetry, and we feel that seeing their own riddles in print will keep that creative spirit burning brightly and proudly.

We hope you enjoy riddling your way through this book as much as we enjoyed reading all the entries.

CONTENTS

Cullen Primary School, Cullen

Ollie McDonald (7)	40
Jessica Helen Crompton (7)	41
Kyan Taylor (6)	42
Callum Stewart (6)	43
Satine Alice Gardon-Haynes (6)	44
Dylan John Cole (6)	45
Alfie Jack (6)	46
Freddy Gill (6)	47
Lauren Innes (7)	48
Maddison Borland (7)	49

Gourdon Primary School, Gourdon

Daniel Matthew Morgan (7)	50
Loukas Pergjoka (7)	51
Charlotte Olivia Morris (7)	52
Alex Littlewood (7)	53
Macy Dorward (7)	54

Helmsdale Primary School, Helmsdale

Zoe Sutherland (8)	55
Alexander Jappy (8)	56
Rachel Hendry (8)	57
Lorna Hope (5)	58
William Maclean Hudson (6)	59
Riley Roberts (6)	60
Skye Sutherland (7)	61
Alan Hudson (7)	62
Caitlyn Sutherland (6)	63
Alex Plommer (5)	64
Lexi Tricker (5)	65
Olly Booth (6)	66
Olivia MacKay (5)	67
Nathan Farrall (7)	68
Andrew Jappy (6)	69
Leah Catherine Sutherland (7)	70
Vaclav Jonak (7)	71

Heriot Primary School, Paisley

Robert Timlin (5)	72
Ava Gordon (5)	73
Kayden McInnes (5)	74
Lauren Anne Casey (5)	75
Ronnie Alexander Jock McAdam (5)	76
Georgia Mairi Ralph (5)	77
Adam Murray (5)	78
Mason Black (6)	79
Oscar James O'Malley (5)	80
Natalie Pauline Czuma (6)	81
Connor McGregor (5)	82

James Aiton Primary School, Cambuslang

Jackson Irons (6)	83
Brodie MacPhee (5)	84
Willow Rose Raggett (6)	85
Calvin Whitfield (6)	86

Sandwood Primary School, Glasgow

Reece Trainer (7)	87
Leah Purewal (6)	88
Elsee Sloan (7)	89
Ava Bowden (7)	90
Callum Alexander Cameron (7)	91
Cameron Fleming (6)	92
Olivia Wilson (7)	93
Amani Ali (7)	94
Sophie Curran (6)	95
Kayla Wright (6)	96
Lucas Law (6)	97
Samyog Kharel (7)	98
Olivia Lewis Bruce (7)	99
Georgia Cassidy (6)	100
Aaliyah Ferguson (6)	101
Abbie Williamson (6)	102
Orla Wilson (6)	103
Frazer Goldie (6)	104

Tyler Gethins (7) — 105
Dina Aenab (6) — 106
Max Jamieson (7) — 107
Maison MacKay (6) — 108
Jamie Brown (7) — 109

Sighthill Primary School, Edinburgh

Hollie Hutchison (7) — 110
Summer Laing (7) — 111
Maddyson Emma Hazell Wright (8) — 112
Lucy Anne Kilkenny (8) — 113
Amelia Murphy (7) — 114
Sophie Moyes (7) — 115
Emilia Mikolajczyk (7) — 116
Cairn Robinson (7) — 117
Phindamandla Tancred Dlamini (7) — 118
Alexandria Blues (7) — 119
Charlie Galli (8) — 120
Mya Shanley (7) — 121
Sally Bondinuba (7) — 122
Tayla Martins (7) — 123
Kevin Stawski (7) — 124
Craig Salmond (7) — 125

St Blane's Primary School, Blantyre

Elvina Thomas (7) — 126
Emma Carney (8) — 127
Quinn Summers (7) — 128
Vhari-Anne Kelly (8) — 129
Devon Olivia (8) — 130
Kara O'Brien (7) — 131
Paityn O'Neill (7) — 132
Kaiden McGurk (7) — 133
Macie Gibson (7) — 134
Jai McBride (7) — 135
Matthew Kelly (7) — 136
Layla Regan (7) — 137
Mary Anderson (8) — 138

Orla Coulter (7) — 139

St Catherine's Primary School, Paisley

Julia Sobanski (7) — 140
Millie Dawson (7) — 141
Freya Isabella McKenna (6) — 142
Mark James Lundie (7) — 143
Lee Stanford Edward Morrison (6) — 144
Catriona Muir Dunbar (6) — 145
Mirryn McCallion (7) — 146

St Ninian's Primary School, Prestwick

Amelia Elliott (7) — 147
Hannah Strachan (6) — 148
Ava Naomi Wooldridge (5) — 149
Lucas Scott (5) — 150
Blair Findleton (5) — 151
Chloe Dunlop (5) — 152
Aiden Reynolds (5) — 153
Amelia Bartkowiak (5) — 154
Bruce Wang (5) — 155
Harry John Dickson (6) — 156
Rjan Dayao (7) — 157
Tanishka Gijeesh (6) — 158

THE POEMS

Petal Power!

I can grow in a garden
I can grow in a pot
I can be just one colour
Maybe I can be lots
I may have loads of petals
Or maybe not
What am I?

Answer: A flower.

Kayla Francis (5)

Under The Sea

I have a sharp fin.
I live under the sea.
I can swim fast.
You can swim with me.
You can swim on my body.
My colours are grey and blue.
What am I?

Answer: A dolphin.

Codie Kirsten Gillies (7)
Antonine Primary School, Drumchapel

Who Am I?

I have a sack.
I have a big, white beard.
I have big boots.
I work with elves.
I come at midnight.
I come on a sleigh.
Who am I?

Answer: Santa Claus.

Tee Jay Traynor (6)
Antonine Primary School, Drumchapel

What Am I?

My tail is poison.
I have eight legs.
I have big fangs.
Some people are scared of me.
I am dark.
I am long.
What am I?

Answer: A scorpion.

Jack Spalding (6)
Antonine Primary School, Drumchapel

Fluffy Ball

I am soft.

I am fluffy.

I am cute.

I am happy.

I am the colour of sand.

I bark.

What am I?

Answer: A dog.

Kyla Honeyman (6)

Antonine Primary School, Drumchapel

What Am I?

I have big doors.
I have big wheels.
I have lights.
I take people to their destinations.
What am I?

Answer: A bus.

Kyle Solman (6)
Antonine Primary School, Drumchapel

A Zoo Animal

I live in the zoo.
I have little, sharp claws.
I have a tail.
I look like a chipmunk.
I have got loads of energy.
I am small.
I like to swing.
I can go into holes.
I can make holes.
I am like a waterfowl because I make holes.
What am I?

Answer: A meerkat.

Lucy Ross (7)
Avenue End Primary School, Garthamlock

What Am I?

My body is stripy.
I am dangerous if you attack me.
My teeth are very sharp.
You can find me in the jungle.
What am I?

Answer: A tiger.

Kailey Bryony (7)
Avenue End Primary School, Garthamlock

The Swift Animal

I love to run as fast as a velociraptor.
I live in the jungle where many trees
and vines grow, it's dark like midnight.
I have hundreds of spots on my body.
I sound like an angry tiger roaring.
I love to eat meat.
I am as clever as a pig.
What am I?

Answer: A cheetah.

Euan Rendall (7)
Baljaffray Primary School, Bearsden

Hoppity

I jump as high as a tree.
I like to eat juicy carrots.
I feel as soft as velvet.
I am really cute and cuddly.
I like hiding in small, dark burrows.
I hear loud noises when I jump about.
I like it when you stroke me gently.
What am I?

Answer: A bunny.

Sophie Smillie (7)
Baljaffray Primary School, Bearsden

Spots

I have spots like a cheetah.
I never sit down.
I am sometimes at the zoo
and sometimes in Africa.
I eat juicy, green leaves.
I do not like loud noises.
I come from Africa.
I have a very long neck like a road.
What am I?

Answer: A giraffe.

Amber Serrels (7)
Baljaffray Primary School, Bearsden

A Fishing Creature

I live in the deepest part of the ocean.
I have a bright light like a nightlight.
My home is in the dark, like at midnight.
It is hard to capture me.
I eat fish like sharks do.
I live as long as twenty-four years.
What am I?

Answer: An angelfish.

Daniyal Ashraf (7)
Baljaffray Primary School, Bearsden

Hoppy

I hop as high as a tree.
I feel as soft as a cotton bud.
I am so cute, you can't resist me.
I am really fun to play with.
You can look after me really well.
I eat orange carrots.
I am as fluffy as a cloud.
What am I?

Answer: A bunny.

Ruby Anna Manton (7)
Baljaffray Primary School, Bearsden

Ferocious

I am very fast like a speedy car.
I am extinct so I no longer live.
I have sharp teeth like a tiger.
I am ferocious like a shark.
I am very dangerous like a lion.
I lived 65,000,000 years ago.
What am I?

Answer: A velociraptor.

Fraser Greer (7)
Baljaffray Primary School, Bearsden

Super Speed

I am as fast as lightning.
Usain Bolt would never beat me in a race.
My colours are red, black or gold.
Ronaldo has eight of me.
My lights are as bright as the sun.
I am a type of car.
What am I?

Answer: A Ferrari.

Jack Shread (7)
Baljaffray Primary School, Bearsden

What Am I?

Kids like to play on me.
I have buttons like a controller.
You buy me in the shops.
I am as comfortable as a sofa.
You get frustrated with me.
I have a screen to play on.
What am I?

Answer: A Nintendo.

Callum Pyke (7)

Baljaffray Primary School, Bearsden

I Love Pets

I am loving like a kiss.
I am as cute as a fluffy kitten.
You take me for a walk.
You find me in a pet shop.
I like food and tasty treats.
I bark like a horn.
What am I?

Answer: A puppy.

Sophia Conway (7)
Baljaffray Primary School, Bearsden

The Big Car

I can carry a lot of junk and trash.
You can drive in me.
I am very fast.
I am a type of car.
I have four wheels.
I can carry little carts.
What am I?

Answer: A truck.

Jake Han (7)
Baljaffray Primary School, Bearsden

Asleep

I am brown, black and white.
I am nocturnal.
I can fly.
I am a bird.
I have big eyes.
I can make a hooting noise.
What am I?

Answer: An owl.

Chloe Eve Taylor (7)
Baljaffray Primary School, Bearsden

Fast With Wheels

I am quite fast.
You can ride me.
I have brakes.
I am known to have a flag.
I race on a track.
I have wheels.
What am I?

Answer: A go-kart.

David Uisdean MacPhee (7)
Baljaffray Primary School, Bearsden

Fly And Shine

I have ears.
I have a mane.
I have legs.
I have wings.
I make a clippety-clop sound.
I have a horn.
What am I?

Answer: A unicorn.

Zoya Abdul-Ghaffar (7)
Baljaffray Primary School, Bearsden

The Nightmare Flyer

I sleep during the day.
I can be seen in dark, spooky caves.
I can fly like a bird.
I can become a Halloween character
in the movies.
I can also eat different things, depending
on the type.
I am the first three letters of a superhero.
What am I?

Answer: A bat.

Finlay McMichael (13)
Cardinal Winning Secondary School, Glasgow

The Carrot Muncher

I bite orange carrots.
I have long, floppy ears.
I sleep in a hutch with straw.
I like to hop.
I am soft and fluffy.
I have a short tail.
What am I?

Answer: A rabbit.

Xingzi Li (13), Jeanette Baidoo, Phillip Moyo (13), Abbie Hennessy & Aiden Jaconelli (13)

Cardinal Winning Secondary School, Glasgow

My Best Friend

I wag my tail.
I love juicy bones.
I am furry and soft.
I like to catch balls.
I love going for walks.
I like to chase cats.
What am I?

Answer: A dog.

Kyle John McGregor (12)
Cardinal Winning Secondary School, Glasgow

Fire-Breather

I breathe hot fire.
I am imaginary, I'm not real.
I can fly in the sky.
I have rough-as-rock scales.
My talons are sharp.
What am I?

Answer: A dragon.

Nicky King (13)

Cardinal Winning Secondary School, Glasgow

The Erupter

I am as hot as the sun.
I have a hole in my head.
Sometimes I explode.
I spit hot liquid.
I am tall like a mountain.
What am I?

Answer: A volcano.

Aiden McSorley (13)
Cardinal Winning Secondary School, Glasgow

Furry And Cute

I have blue eyes.
I have black and white fur.
I like to be clapped and hugged.
I have floppy ears and I am fluffy.
What am I?

Answer: A husky dog.

Marc Hamilton (13)
Cardinal Winning Secondary School, Glasgow

A White Wanderer

I lose my coat every year.
I might be part of your clothing collection.
I got lost in the Bible.
You might find milk or cheese in the shop.
You might find lots of my offspring
in New Zealand.
I am owned by a shepherd.
What am I?

Answer: A sheep.

Ivan Evbayiro (6), Jared & Louise Harkins

Corpus Christi Primary School, Glasgow

Brilliant And Blue

I am dotty and wrinkly.
I can be used to make smoothies.
My skin is blue.
I have many vitamins inside of me.
I have a prickly top.
I have a juicy core.
What am I?

Answer: A blueberry.

Quinn Carrigan (6) & Dylan Iremonger
Corpus Christi Primary School, Glasgow

Animal Adventure

I like napping in the sun.
I am soft and furry.
I like eating fish for dinner.
I am excellent company.
I love to hunt outside.
I have baby kittens.
What am I?

Answer: A cat.

Zara King (6), Reece Robertson, Omer & Ayden-Jase

Corpus Christi Primary School, Glasgow

Colours Galore

I like copying noises.
I have dangerous, sharp feet.
I can have as many colours as a rainbow.
I crunch seeds with my beak.
I am as fluffy as a sheep.
What am I?

Answer: A parrot.

Luke McGrath (6), Daniel, Haidar & Millie Fiona Harte
Corpus Christi Primary School, Glasgow

A Royal Beast

I have four strong legs.
I can have a very loud roar.
I have a very big mane.
I am very furry.
I have big, sharp claws.
I am a meat eater.
What am I?

Answer: A lion.

Lucas Zhang (6) & Jacob Richardson
Corpus Christi Primary School, Glasgow

Tame And Wild

I am a fast runner.
I have a big dog nose.
I can be found in the African safari.
I have long ears to kill flies.
I have stripes.
What am I?

Answer: A zebra.

Bean Hiso (6), Connor Baird & Danish
Corpus Christi Primary School, Glasgow

Hanging On The Wall

I have two body parts.
People are scared of me.
I am not an insect.
I eat delicious flies for my dinner.
I make silk.
I lay eggs and wrap them in silk.
I have eight hairy legs.
I have six or eight eyes.
I can come in different colours.
What am I?

Answer: A spider.

Jodie McDonald (7)
Crudie Primary School, Crudie

Silk Spinner

I have eight hairy legs.
I lay eggs.
I have silk to make webs.
I eat yummy insects.
I fight, I hunt, I bite.
I am an arachnid.
What am I?

Answer: A spider.

Michael Lee Sorby (8)
Crudie Primary School, Crudie

Wriggle Jiggle

I have up to ten hearts.
I have a peach saddle.
I lay many eggs.
I am not an insect.
I have no eyes.
I am an underground farmer.
What am I?

Answer: A worm.

Joss McLaren (5)
Crudie Primary School, Crudie

Creepy-Crawly

I have two body parts.
I like to scare people.
I am not an insect.
I eat flies.
I have eight legs.
I have eight or six eyes.
What am I?

Answer: A spider.

Rachael Brennan (7)
Crudie Primary School, Crudie

Wiggle Wriggle

I live underground.
I don't like the light.
I have a saddle.
I wiggle and wriggle.
I am grey and pink.
What am I?

Answer: A worm.

Leigh Elizabeth Malarky (5)
Crudie Primary School, Crudie

Creepy-Crawly

I have eight legs.
I eat flies.
I make webs.
I am not an insect.
I have more than two eyes.
What am I?

Answer: A spider.

Robert Jay Sorby (6)
Crudie Primary School, Crudie

Web

I eat flies.
I can make webs.
Some of me are poisonous.
You get me in Great Britain.
I am hairy.
I have eight legs.
What am I?

Answer: A spider.

Ollie McDonald (7)
Cullen Primary School, Cullen

Slimy

I have a shell.
I eat leaves.
I am slimy.
I am brown.
I have two eyes.
I don't have arms and legs.
What am I?

Answer: A snail.

Jessica Helen Crompton (7)
Cullen Primary School, Cullen

Slithery

I have five hearts.
When I get chopped in half, two are born.
I like soil.
I live in soil.
I dig tunnels.
What am I?

Answer: A worm.

Kyan Taylor (6)
Cullen Primary School, Cullen

Slimy

I am slimy.
I have long eyes.
I have a shell.
I am really long.
I am really slow.
I have no legs.
What am I?

Answer: A snail.

Callum Stewart (6)
Cullen Primary School, Cullen

Buzz

I have black and yellow stripes.
I eat nectar.
I can sting.
I can sting one time.
After I sting, I die.
What am I?

Answer: A bee.

Satine Alice Gardon-Haynes (6)
Cullen Primary School, Cullen

Scratch

I have two body parts.
I have eight legs.
I have four eyes.
I eat flies.
I make webs.
What am I?

Answer: A spider.

Dylan John Cole (6)
Cullen Primary School, Cullen

Strong

I have wings.
I have strong legs.
I have a stinger on me.
I can dig.
I have six legs.
What am I?

Answer: An ant.

Alfie Jack (6)
Cullen Primary School, Cullen

Poisonous

I have eight legs.
I have four eyes.
I am poisonous.
I am fast.
I have sharp teeth.
What am I?

Answer: A spider.

Freddy Gill (6)
Cullen Primary School, Cullen

Wriggle

I have no legs.
I have a shell.
I eat leaves.
I can slither.
I have no arms.
What am I?

Answer: A snail.

Lauren Innes (7)
Cullen Primary School, Cullen

Flyer

I can fly.
I have orange eyes.
I have long wings.
I have four arms.
What am I?

Answer: A dragonfly.

Maddison Borland (7)
Cullen Primary School, Cullen

Going Really Fast

I am yellow, some say golden.
I destroy blocks coloured golden.
I hurt the pesky pigs!
I go out at superspeed.
Some people think I eat seeds.
I have a black tail.
I have black hair.
Who am I?

Answer: Chuck (The Adventures of Chuck).

Daniel Matthew Morgan (7)
Gourdon Primary School, Gourdon

Caught In Webs

I climb on big buildings.
I am a superhero and a saviour.
I shoot webs out of my hands.
I swing on buildings and walk on them.
I don't have eight legs.
I have two legs!
Who am I?

Answer: Spider-Man.

Loukas Pergjoka (7)
Gourdon Primary School, Gourdon

So Sweet

I am tasty.
I get licked and sometimes sucked.
I am extremely creamy.
I am super, super, super special.
I am wonderful with cream.
I am extra huge and super delicious.
What am I?

Answer: An ice cream.

Charlotte Olivia Morris (7)
Gourdon Primary School, Gourdon

Speeding Stunts

Some are big, some are small,
Some are green, some are blue,
I have one, do you?
Some have pedals, some don't,
There are different types,
Some have motors, some do not,
What am I?

Answer: A bike.

Alex Littlewood (7)
Gourdon Primary School, Gourdon

Very Sparkly

I am very magical and beautiful.
You will never see me.
I am invisible.
I am very sparkly and nice.
My fur is very soft.
What am I?

Answer: A unicorn.

Macy Dorward (7)
Gourdon Primary School, Gourdon

The Cutie

I live on a big farm.
I eat green grass every day.
I have a fluffy coat.
I like playing with my friends.
I have four legs with fluff on them.
When I grow up, I make this noise -
Baaa!
What am I?

Answer: A sheep.

Zoe Sutherland (8)
Helmsdale Primary School, Helmsdale

Transporter

It pulls things.
You see it on the croft.
It has tyres that give it grip.
The back tyres drive, the front tyres turn.
It is mostly seen in red and green.
It is good in mud.
What is it?

Answer: A tractor.

Alexander Jappy (8)
Helmsdale Primary School, Helmsdale

The Flowers Lover

You can see me on flowers.
I am colourful.
My wings break when you hold me.
I love flying up in the sky.
Some think I am horrible.
I am scared of people.
What am I?

Answer: A butterfly.

Rachel Hendry (8)
Helmsdale Primary School, Helmsdale

Party Piece

I am something to eat.
I am something tasty.
You eat me at parties.
I am covered with icing.
You can put candles on me.
I can be different shapes.
What am I?

Answer: A cake.

Lorna Hope (5)
Helmsdale Primary School, Helmsdale

Twister

It is shiny.
It turns in a hole.
It can be big or small.
It opens doors and cars.
It is made of metal.
In books, it can be magic.
What is it?

Answer: A key.

William Maclean Hudson (6)
Helmsdale Primary School, Helmsdale

The Jumper

I eat juicy carrots.
I eat hay.
I like to jump over obstacles.
People can ride on me.
I like to race.
I go *neigh!*
What am I?

Answer: A horse.

Riley Roberts (6)
Helmsdale Primary School, Helmsdale

The Shiner

I live in the sky.
I zoom across the sky.
I shine bright.
I fly in the sky at night.
I am twinkly.
You can't count me.
What am I?

Answer: A star.

Skye Sutherland (7)
Helmsdale Primary School, Helmsdale

The Hopper

I live in a hole.
I have floppy ears.
I have a fluffy coat.
I like jumping.
I like grass.
I make a good pet.
What am I?

Answer: A bunny rabbit.

Alan Hudson (7)
Helmsdale Primary School, Helmsdale

The Pedal Machine

It has two wheels.
It has a seat.
It has two pedals.
It goes fast.
It sometimes has a bell.
It has handlebars.
What is it?

Answer: A bicycle.

Caitlyn Sutherland (6)
Helmsdale Primary School, Helmsdale

The Runner

It jumps high.
It likes to swim.
It runs fast.
It has four legs.
It helps people.
It says *woof, woof!*
What is it?

Answer: A dog.

Alex Plommer (5)
Helmsdale Primary School, Helmsdale

Spirit

I live in a field.
I have four legs.
I have a tail.
I eat grass.
You can ride on me.
I say *neigh!*
What am I?

Answer: A horse.

Lexi Tricker (5)
Helmsdale Primary School, Helmsdale

Fluffy

You find me on the farm.
I eat grass.
I am fluffy.
I am smelly.
I have lambs.
I go *baaa!*
What am I?

Answer: A sheep.

Olly Booth (6)
Helmsdale Primary School, Helmsdale

The Rainbow Flash

I am gentle.
I am colourful.
I have four legs.
I am magic.
I can fly.
I have a golden horn.
What am I?

Answer: A unicorn.

Olivia MacKay (5)
Helmsdale Primary School, Helmsdale

The Mad Runner

I am vicious.
I am crazy.
I am fast.
I lick you.
I go *woof!*
I run on four legs.
What am I?

Answer: A dog.

Nathan Farrall (7)
Helmsdale Primary School, Helmsdale

The Turner Opener

I turn.
I am made of metal.
I keep things safe.
I am found on lockers.
I can turn cars on.
What am I?

Answer: A key.

Andrew Jappy (6)
Helmsdale Primary School, Helmsdale

Clippy-Clop

I go *neigh!*
I live on a farm.
I eat grass.
I live in a barn.
I eat hay.
What am I?

Answer: A horse.

Leah Catherine Sutherland (7)
Helmsdale Primary School, Helmsdale

Changer

I have a long tongue.
I can change colours.
I have a long tail.
I live in Australia.
What am I?

Answer: A lizard.

Vaclav Jonak (7)
Helmsdale Primary School, Helmsdale

Cool Food

I come in different colours.
I can come in a cone.
You can put different sauces on me.
Some people lick me and I can't run away.
I come in different flavours.
You can use me to cool down.
What am I?

Answer: An ice cream.

Robert Timlin (5)
Heriot Primary School, Paisley

Stripy

I have black and orange stripes.
I live in the jungle.
I hunt for food.
I have a load roar.
Sometimes people are scared of me.
I can be a bit naughty.
What am I?

Answer: A tiger.

Ava Gordon (5)
Heriot Primary School, Paisley

Roar

I have terribly sharp claws.
People are scared of me.
I have sharp teeth.
I have stripes.
I am dangerous but fluffy.
I have a tail.
What am I?

Answer: A tiger.

Kayden McInnes (5)
Heriot Primary School, Paisley

Galloping

I come in different colours.
I eat grass and hay.
I am fluffy.
You can ride on me.
I can jump over things.
I love to eat carrots.
What am I?

Answer: A horse.

Lauren Anne Casey (5)
Heriot Primary School, Paisley

Howl

I am furry.
I go out when it is dark.
I live in the woods.
I once dressed up as a gran.
I live in a pack.
I like to howl.
What am I?

Answer: A wolf.

Ronnie Alexander Jock McAdam (5)
Heriot Primary School, Paisley

In The Jungle

I have a big mane.
I am yellow.
I like meat.
I have a tail.
Sometimes I am naughty.
I roar.
What am I?

Answer: A lion.

Georgia Mairi Ralph (5)
Heriot Primary School, Paisley

Spotty

I am tall.
I like leaves.
I walk slow.
My tail wiggles.
I have spots.
I have two ears.
What am I?

Answer: A giraffe.

Adam Murray (5)
Heriot Primary School, Paisley

Cheeky

I climb trees.
I am brown.
I am cheeky.
I am in Africa.
I have a long tail.
What am I?

Answer: A monkey.

Mason Black (6)
Heriot Primary School, Paisley

Out Of Africa

I am fast.
I have spots.
I live in Africa.
I like to eat meat.
I hunt.
What am I?

Answer: A cheetah.

Oscar James O'Malley (5)
Heriot Primary School, Paisley

Stripes

I have stripes.
I am white and I am black.
I look like a horse.
I have ears.
What am I?

Answer: A zebra.

Natalie Pauline Czuma (6)

Heriot Primary School, Paisley

Fast

I have spots.
I am fast.
I have long legs.
I am loud.
What am I?

Answer: A cheetah.

Connor McGregor (5)
Heriot Primary School, Paisley

What Am I?

I am big.
I punch my chest when I am angry.
I have black fur.
I don't have a tail.
I have little ears.
What am I?

Answer: A gorilla.

Jackson Irons (6)
James Aiton Primary School, Cambuslang

What Am I?

I have a long body.
I slither.
I have a big head.
I have no legs.
My skin is green.
What am I?

Answer: A snake.

Brodie MacPhee (5)
James Aiton Primary School, Cambuslang

What Am I?

I have a mane.
I have yellow skin.
I have claws.
I have a tail.
I roar.
What am I?

Answer: A lion.

Willow Rose Raggett (6)
James Aiton Primary School, Cambuslang

What Is It?

It is grey.
It has big jaws.
It lives in a waterhole.
It has square teeth.
What is it?

Answer: A hippo.

Calvin Whitfield (6)

James Aiton Primary School, Cambuslang

Riddle Me This

In the day I am nice and not frightening but in the night I don't survive.
At 6am it is time to leave before we get frozen.
I am made out of parts of metal.
I better get out of here before I do this...
Kaa!
Who am I?

Answer: Foxy.

Reece Trainer (7)
Sandwood Primary School, Glasgow

Where Could I Be...?

I can see the yellow sand.
I can see the cold, blue water.
I can see children playing with buckets
and spades.
I can see a beach ball.
I can see an umbrella.
What am I?

Answer: *The beach.*

Leah Purewal (6)
Sandwood Primary School, Glasgow

The Riddle

I am cute.
I can jump high.
People think I am cuddly.
We stay in a group.
I live in the wild.
When I jump, I can see trees and lots more.
What am I?

Answer: A bunny.

Elsee Sloan (7)

Sandwood Primary School, Glasgow

Guess Who?

I love red, green and white.
I love giving presents.
I have a beard.
I wear a special suit.
I can go up in the air.
I go through chimneys.
Who am I?

Answer: Santa.

Ava Bowden (7)
Sandwood Primary School, Glasgow

Guess Who...?

I have wings.
I live in the sea.
I eat fish food.
I can escape from sharks quickly.
I am short.
I can pretend to be a sausage.
What am I?

Answer: A flying fish.

Callum Alexander Cameron (7)
Sandwood Primary School, Glasgow

Guess What?

I have red spikes.
I have a small head.
I have a big body.
I have spikes on my tail.
I have a yellow body.
I am a herbivore.
What am I?

Answer: A stegosaurus.

Cameron Fleming (6)
Sandwood Primary School, Glasgow

The Mystery Riddle

It is loud.

There is a stage.

There are lots of lights.

There is lots of food.

There are lots of people.

There is music playing.

What is it?

Answer: A party.

Olivia Wilson (7)

Sandwood Primary School, Glasgow

Guess What?

I eat bananas.
I go *oo, oo, ah, ah!*
I am brown.
I climb trees.
My tail hangs upside down on trees.
I scratch.
What am I?

Answer: A monkey.

Amani Ali (7)
Sandwood Primary School, Glasgow

Guess What?

I have black and orange stripes.
I live in the jungle.
I have sharp teeth.
I have a cub in my tummy.
I can run fast.
I eat meat.
What am I?

Answer: A tiger.

Sophie Curran (6)
Sandwood Primary School, Glasgow

Kayla's Riddle

There are lots of animals.
I am far away.
Lots of people come to visit.
People come to look at animals.
I am busy.
I am outside.
What am I?

Answer: A zoo.

Kayla Wright (6)
Sandwood Primary School, Glasgow

The Riddle

I am big.
Kids can bounce on me.
Kids have fun on me.
I need to be outside.
I might be in your garden.
No adults allowed!
What am I?

Answer: A trampoline.

Lucas Law (6)

Sandwood Primary School, Glasgow

The Riddle

I sing at Five Nights at Freddy's.
I have a guitar.
I have a microphone.
I am golden.
I have golden ears.
I am big.
Who am I?

Answer: Spring Bonnie.

Samyog Kharel (7)
Sandwood Primary School, Glasgow

I Am Healthy

You can eat me.
I am red and green.
You need to put me in the fridge.
I am healthy.
I have got seeds.
I taste yummy.
What am I?

Answer: A watermelon.

Olivia Lewis Bruce (7)
Sandwood Primary School, Glasgow

Guess What?

I am colourful.
I have a horn.
I have a family.
My family are nice to me.
I am magical.
I live with my mum and dad.
What am I?

Answer: A unicorn.

Georgia Cassidy (6)
Sandwood Primary School, Glasgow

The Riddle

I am very small.
I will hatch from an egg.
I am yellow.
I have wings and a beak.
I am quiet.
I will chirp and cheep.
What am I?

Answer: A chick.

Aaliyah Ferguson (6)
Sandwood Primary School, Glasgow

The Riddle

I have a horn.
I am colourful.
I am in my teacher's class.
Everyone loves me.
I am magical.
I have four legs.
What am I?

Answer: A unicorn.

Abbie Williamson (6)
Sandwood Primary School, Glasgow

Guess What?

I live in the woods.
I can climb trees.
I am brown.
I like bananas.
I can swing from the trees.
I can climb fast.
What am I?

Answer: A monkey.

Orla Wilson (6)
Sandwood Primary School, Glasgow

The Riddle

I am the king of the jungle.
I can roar.
I am golden.
My babies are called cubs.
I have big paws.
I eat meat.
What am I?

Answer: A lion.

Frazer Goldie (6)
Sandwood Primary School, Glasgow

Guess What?

I am orange, black and white.
I eat meat.
I have a bushy tail.
I can run fast.
I am small.
I live in a den.
What am I?

Answer: A fox.

Tyler Gethins (7)
Sandwood Primary School, Glasgow

A Pet

I have a tail.
I have four legs.
I have two ears.
I have sharp nails.
I have sharp teeth.
I can run fast.
What am I?

Answer: A cat.

Dina Aenab (6)
Sandwood Primary School, Glasgow

The Riddle

I have two wheels.
Do not crash me!
I am really fast.
You can go on me.
I can blow up.
I am noisy.
What am I?

Answer: A motorbike.

Max Jamieson (7)
Sandwood Primary School, Glasgow

Guess What?

I am scary.
I am orange with black stripes.
I am big.
I will eat you.
I can roar.
I am in a cage.
What am I?

Answer: A tiger.

Maison MacKay (6)
Sandwood Primary School, Glasgow

Guess What?

I eat meat.
I can climb trees.
I am yellow.
I can hide.
I can run fast.
What am I?

Answer: A lion.

Jamie Brown (7)
Sandwood Primary School, Glasgow

Wood Sneaker

Someone sneaky, someone hidden.
I am hidden really well.
I live in the woods.
I live with my cubs.
I eat what I find.
I have a puffy tail.
My face is red, orange and white.
I am really cute.
I am not a pet.
I am really rare.
What am I?

Answer: A fox.

Hollie Hutchison (7)
Sighthill Primary School, Edinburgh

The Ball Runner

I run a lot.
I am small and I am cute.
Everyone loves me.
I have pointy ears.
I can be any colour like black, white,
grey, blonde or ginger.
Sometimes people give me a walk.
What am I?

Answer: A chihuahua.

Summer Laing (7)
Sighthill Primary School, Edinburgh

The Cute Pet

I am as cute as a cat.
I bounce like a bunny.
I have black spots all over.
My tail is long.
When I chase my tail, I look like a zebra.
What am I?

Answer: A Dalmatian.

Maddyson Emma Hazell Wright (8)
Sighthill Primary School, Edinburgh

Best Flyer

I am as small as a worm.
Some people like me.
I am a good flyer.
I am colourful.
Sometimes I am not colourful.
I am nice and colourful and beautiful.
What am I?

Answer: A butterfly.

Lucy Anne Kilkenny (8)
Sighthill Primary School, Edinburgh

Night Watcher

I look in rubbish bins.
I live in the woods.
I run when I see you.
I hunt for me and my cubs.
I lurk in the pitch-black night.
I hide behind the trees.
What am I?

Answer: A fox.

Amelia Murphy (7)
Sighthill Primary School, Edinburgh

Mr Mean

I am rude.
I am like Darth Vader.
I hate babies.
I am mean.
I am a monster machine.
I think I am handsome.
What am I?

Answer: A villain.

Sophie Moyes (7)
Sighthill Primary School, Edinburgh

USA Rules!

I am famous.
I live in the USA.
I am a president.
I say, "China."
I have beautiful, blonde hair.
Who am I?

Answer: Donald Trump.

Emilia Mikolajczyk (7)
Sighthill Primary School, Edinburgh

Milk Drinker

I drink milk.
I am brown.
I am cute.
I have whiskers.
I am smaller than a dog.
I am scared of dogs.
What am I?

Answer: A cat.

Cairn Robinson (7)
Sighthill Primary School, Edinburgh

The Wild Beast

I lurk in the dark.
I eat what I find.
I am deadly and fearsome.
I have teeth as sharp as a chainsaw.
What am I?

Answer: A werewolf.

Phindamandla Tancred Dlamini (7)
Sighthill Primary School, Edinburgh

Book Madness

She loves books.
She wears a necklace and earrings.
She likes unicorns, she has them
everywhere.
Who is she?

Answer: Miss Allison.

Alexandria Blues (7)
Sighthill Primary School, Edinburgh

The Killer Of Fire

I am as hot as the boiling sun.
I hate the water.
I live in a volcano.
I can erupt at any second.
What am I?

Answer: Lava.

Charlie Galli (8)
Sighthill Primary School, Edinburgh

People Sitter

I am bigger than people but smaller than a lamp post.
I am red.
I have a lot of people inside.
What am I?

Answer: A bus.

Mya Shanley (7)
Sighthill Primary School, Edinburgh

The Special Person

I am a lady.
I wave.
I talk posh.
I have a lovely car.
I wear special clothes.
Who am I?

Answer: The Queen.

Sally Bondinuba (7)
Sighthill Primary School, Edinburgh

Haunted House

I'm see-through.
I go *ooooh!*
I'm white.
Last of all, I am scary.
What am I?

Answer: A ghost.

Tayla Martins (7)
Sighthill Primary School, Edinburgh

The Highest Jumper

I jump every day.
I collect carrots.
My home is a hole.
I jump to go fast.
What am I?

Answer: A bunny.

Kevin Stawski (7)
Sighthill Primary School, Edinburgh

Cutie Pie

I look cute.
I like rolling in the grass.
I have a lead.
I go for a walk.
What am I?

Answer: A dog.

Craig Salmond (7)
Sighthill Primary School, Edinburgh

Who Am I?

I am the sister of Elvina.
I have met Shreya in a lot of places.
I love playing inside and outside.
I love my mum and dad.
I like playing with my sisters.
I have learnt lots of things,
like my first words.
I am able to walk and crawl
and climb the stairs.
I am able to get out of bed.
I am a cheeky monkey.
Who am I?

Answer: My baby sister.

Elvina Thomas (7)
St Blane's Primary School, Blantyre

What Is It?

It's very arty.
It's got colours bright and dark.
You can make brilliant pictures with it.
The pictures can make you a superstar!
What is it?

Answer: A paint set.

Emma Carney (8)
St Blane's Primary School, Blantyre

What Am I?

I am sharp.
I can be all different colours.
I am used to write.
I am also used to colour in.
I can be rubbed out easily.
What am I?

Answer: A pencil.

Quinn Summers (7)
St Blane's Primary School, Blantyre

What Am I?

I live in the forest.
I scare people away.
I hunt for my prey.
I am scary.
I eat animals.
I eat humans.
What am I?

Answer: A Monster Girl.

Vhari-Anne Kelly (8)
St Blane's Primary School, Blantyre

Underwater

It is a fruit.
It has something soft in it.
I use it too.
It is on TV too.
What is it?

Answer: SpongeBob's pineapple house.

Devon Olivia (8)
St Blane's Primary School, Blantyre

I'm A Fit, Sleepy Girl Who Runs

I have spots.
For me to get fit, I run for a bit.
When I run out of energy, I rest for a while.
What am I?

Answer: A cheetah.

Kara O'Brien (7)
St Blane's Primary School, Blantyre

What Am I?

I am brown.
I am tall.
I am wide.
I have bricks.
I have a car.
I have a hut.
What am I?

Answer: A mansion.

Paityn O'Neill (7)
St Blane's Primary School, Blantyre

What Am I?

I am an animal.
I live under the sea.
My name starts with a 'T'.
What am I?

Answer: A tiger shark.

Kaiden McGurk (7)

St Blane's Primary School, Blantyre

What Am I?

I am a pink animal.
I am from Africa.
I have long legs and a long beak.
What am I?

Answer: A flamingo.

Macie Gibson (7)

St Blane's Primary School, Blantyre

What Is It?

It is grey.
It has a horn.
It has four legs.
It has a tail.
What is it?

Answer: A rhino.

Jai McBride (7)
St Blane's Primary School, Blantyre

What Am I?

I am a shark.
I am fast.
My name starts with an 'M'.
What am I?

Answer: A mako shark.

Matthew Kelly (7)
St Blane's Primary School, Blantyre

What Am I?

I am not human.
I don't have feet.
I have lots of seats.
What am I?

Answer: A house.

Layla Regan (7)
St Blane's Primary School, Blantyre

What Am I?

It is yellow.
It is really pretty.
It grows.
What is it?

Answer: A flower.

Mary Anderson (8)
St Blane's Primary School, Blantyre

What Am I?

I am a bird.
I am also a human.
I have hair.
What am I?

Answer: A girl.

Orla Coulter (7)
St Blane's Primary School, Blantyre

The Sea Girl

I have a beautiful, shiny tail.
I am as beautiful as a shell.
I have beautiful, pink locks.
I love to dance and swim.
I have eyes as blue as the sky.
I have a tail like a fish.
What am I?

Answer: A mermaid.

Julia Sobanski (7)
St Catherine's Primary School, Paisley

The Pink Bird

I walk in the long, green grass.
I am as fluffy as a teddy and as pink
as pigs' skin.
My neck is as long as a giraffe.
My legs are long and thin.
I eat food from the sea.
What am I?

Answer: A flamingo.

Millie Dawson (7)
St Catherine's Primary School, Paisley

The Girl Who Lives In The Ocean

I have hair as red as fire.
I have a tail as long as a snake.
I dive deep down into the blue ocean.
I sit and watch people play.
I swim fast with my sea friends.
What am I?

Answer: A mermaid.

Freya Isabella McKenna (6)
St Catherine's Primary School, Paisley

Monkey Food

I am the shape of a half moon.
I am yellow like the sun.
I am hard on the outside but soft
in the middle.
I am tasty like sweets.
I can be peeled.
What am I?

Answer: A banana.

Mark James Lundie (7)
St Catherine's Primary School, Paisley

What Am I?

I am as yellow as a banana.
My skin is as fluffy as a rug.
I am as loud as a racket.
I eat animals that I hunt.
My hair is as orange as the sun.
What am I?

Answer: A lion.

Lee Stanford Edward Morrison (6)
St Catherine's Primary School, Paisley

The Magical Creature

I am white like the shining moon.
I like to learn about Earth.
I have a pointy horn on my head.
I have dazzling, white wings.
What am I?

Answer: A unicorn.

Catriona Muir Dunbar (6)
St Catherine's Primary School, Paisley

The Flying Rainbow

I start all wrapped up.
I have colourful wings.
I fly from flower to flower.
I like to drink honey from a yummy flower.
What am I?

Answer: A butterfly.

Mirryn McCallion (7)
St Catherine's Primary School, Paisley

Hoppy

I am as white as a fluffy cloud.
I live underground.
I can jump really high.
I have long ears.
I am really fluffy.
My eyes are as green as grass.
What am I?

Answer: A rabbit.

Amelia Elliott (7)
St Ninian's Primary School, Prestwick

Long And Floppy

I am soft.
I am grey.
I am very good at jumping.
I have long, floppy ears.
I have bendy legs.
I am fluffy.
What am I?

Answer: A rabbit.

Hannah Strachan (6)
St Ninian's Primary School, Prestwick

Fluffy Thing

I am cute.
I like to have long naps.
I am small and soft.
I am grey.
I am a good jumper.
I can lick you.
What am I?

Answer: A cat.

Ava Naomi Wooldridge (5)
St Ninian's Primary School, Prestwick

Buzz

I get pollen.
I am an insect.
I am a good flyer.
I have wings.
I sting people.
I make honey.
What am I?

Answer: A bee.

Lucas Scott (5)
St Ninian's Primary School, Prestwick

I Am Juicy

I have tiny seeds.
I am red.
I am big.
I am juicy.
I am gobbled up.
I am very healthy.
What am I?

Answer: An apple.

Blair Findleton (5)
St Ninian's Primary School, Prestwick

Fluffy

I hop crazily.
I am fluffy.
I have long ears.
I am cute.
I am cuddly.
I am grey.
What am I?

Answer: A rabbit.

Chloe Dunlop (5)
St Ninian's Primary School, Prestwick

Big Thing

I am big.
I am fast.
I am rainbow-coloured.
I have glass on me.
I have air in me.
What am I?

Answer: A car.

Aiden Reynolds (5)
St Ninian's Primary School, Prestwick

Red And Juicy

I have seeds in my middle.
I am juicy.
I am as bright as fire.
I can be gobbled up.
What am I?

Answer: An apple.

Amelia Bartkowiak (5)
St Ninian's Primary School, Prestwick

Pedal

I have wheels and I can move.
I have flashing lights.
I have a brake.
I have a chain.
What am I?

Answer: A bike.

Bruce Wang (5)
St Ninian's Primary School, Prestwick

The Mighty Thing

I am bad.
I am bright.
I am fast.
I am yellow.
I am mighty.
I am scary.
What am I?

Answer: A lion.

Harry John Dickson (6)
St Ninian's Primary School, Prestwick

Roar

I have a long tail.
I have big feet.
I have a big head.
I have a big roar.
What am I?

Answer: A lion.

Rjan Dayao (7)
St Ninian's Primary School, Prestwick

Airport Toys

I can fly.
I can take bags.
I am colourful and sparkly.
What am I?

Answer: An aeroplane.

Tanishka Gijeesh (6)
St Ninian's Primary School, Prestwick

YoungWriters
Est.1991

YOUNG WRITERS INFORMATION

We hope you have enjoyed reading this book – and that you will continue to in the coming years.

If you're a young writer who enjoys reading and creative writing, or the parent of an enthusiastic poet or story writer, do visit our website **www.youngwriters.co.uk**. Here you will find free competitions, workshops and games, as well as recommended reads, a poetry glossary and our blog.

If you would like to order further copies of this book, or any of our other titles, then please give us a call or visit **www.youngwriters.co.uk**.

Young Writers
Remus House
Coltsfoot Drive
Peterborough
PE2 9BF
(01733) 890066
info@youngwriters.co.uk